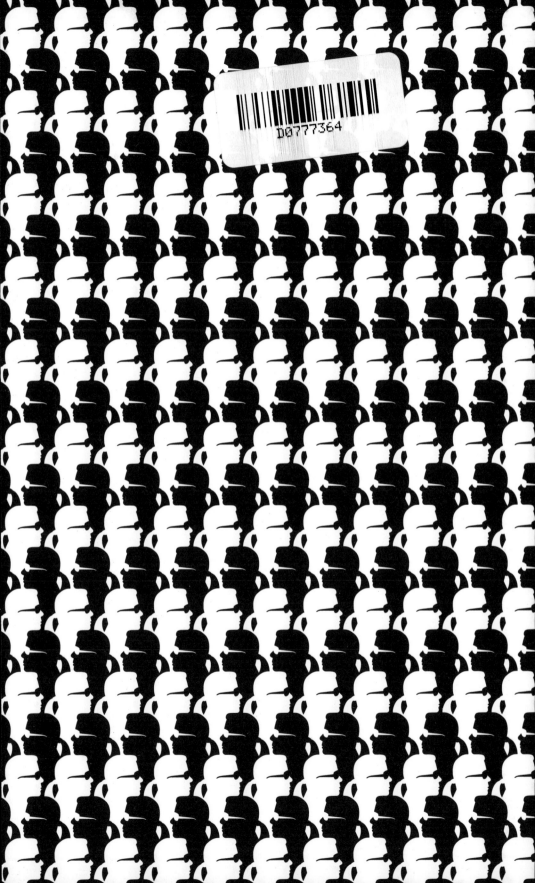

THE WORLD
ACCORDING TO

Karl

THE WORLD
ACCORDING TO

Karl

THE WIT AND WISDOM OF KARL LAGERFELD

Edited by
Jean-Christophe Napias
Sandrine Gulbenkian

Foreword by
Patrick Mauriès

Illustrations by
Charles Ameline

 Thames & Hudson

First published in the United Kingdom in 2013 by
Thames & Hudson Ltd, 181A High Holborn,
London WC1V 7QX

British Library Cataloguing-in-Publication Data
A catalogue record for this book is available from
the British Library

ISBN 978-0-500-51711-6

Printed and bound in China by C & C Offset Printing Co. Ltd

To find out about all our publications, please visit **www.thamesandhudson.com**.
There you can subscribe to our e-newsletter, browse or download our current
catalogue, and buy any titles that are in print.

CONTENTS

THE IRREGULAR

Anyone who has spent time, however brief, with Karl Lagerfeld – the 'real' Karl Lagerfeld, the one who has long been hidden behind those dark glasses, seeing but not being seen – knows him to be fanatical about the present. But anyone acquainted with the other Karl Lagerfeld, or one of the others, may also know that he is intimately familiar with the world of the ladies who hosted the salons of eighteenth-century Paris (Madame du Deffand, Mademoiselle de Lespinasse), and of La Princesse Palatine, correspondent of Descartes a century earlier. Their letters, their way of life, their rare intellectual sophistication have set his imagination alight.

To meet Karl Lagerfeld, or even simply to see him on screen, is to know his incredible presence of mind. He is a master of the cut and thrust that once defined the salons, and which he seems to have inherited effortlessly from his mother, whom he mentions often (as we shall see), and who was possessed of a wit as razor-sharp as her son's. Never short of a lightning response – a stranger to *l'esprit d'escalier* – his repartee can be breathtaking. It doesn't take long, in his presence, to be reduced to faltering inarticulacy.

The glittering conversation of the salons has been silent for some time now. The last embers of this secular tradition arguably died at the end of the 1960s, at the same time as the demise of figures such as the de Noailles and the de Vilmorins, society figures with their roots in the nineteenth century. It was also in the 1960s that new lifestyles began to emerge, together with new kinds of social interaction, cultural registers and, not coincidentally, the sort of ready-to-wear clothing that Karl Lagerfeld embraced from the beginning and turned to good advantage in the years that followed.

Today we live in the era of the 'global salon', where 'sharing', rather than conversation, fills the ether; where one novelty chases another from one moment to the next, and where one must always

be wired in. No one thrives better in this age than Karl Lagerfeld, our faithful reader of Mademoiselle Aïssé's letters. He participates more for fun than anything else, it seems, responding liberally and multilingually to the daily demands via the press or the airwaves from the clamouring media whose playthings we are. Words are cast out to anyone and everyone, tirelessly picked up, polished and finally amplified across the planet, with force enough to ruffle the hair of a president, and yet fated to turn into the dust of the present. But this does not displease our hero, who cares nothing for posterity, and who has no other wish, he'd have us believe, than to let his utterances scatter and fade away.

Faint at the thought, the editors of this volume have set about gathering these statements that might otherwise have disappeared, leaving nothing more than a fleeting smile. The results presented here make up a sort of indirect self-portrait, one facet (or chapter) at a time, the personal statement of a life view that, for all its fragmentary nature, gives us a detailed and captivating picture of a true 'irregular' (to borrow the word once famously used to describe Mademoiselle Chanel). The reader will have to judge how faithful this portrait is, and to size up the intelligence and complexity of a character who seeks less to defy convention than to assert his own values and ideas of correctness. His cardinal virtue is clear-sightedness, stripped of delusions – including, as far as possible, self-delusion. Only such a master of the masque and the feint as Karl Lagerfeld could uphold so demanding an ideal.

The various participants in the creation of this book have a common passion: an invincible and immoderate love of the printed word. Modern, ultramodern, Karl Lagerfeld continues to persist, it is said, in buying his books in threes: one to read, one to cut up, and the third to send to one of his libraries. Albeit less liberally, the editors are themselves concerned with the business of the book, in every sense, while I have myself made books my *raison d'être*; not a day passes for any of us that we do not add to our treasure trove. Therefore it seemed inevitable, as soon as the idea arose, to render homage to this singularly free spirit and proponent of strong opinions in the form of a book – a book that he might add to the top of the stacks that surround and inspire him.

Patrick Mauriès

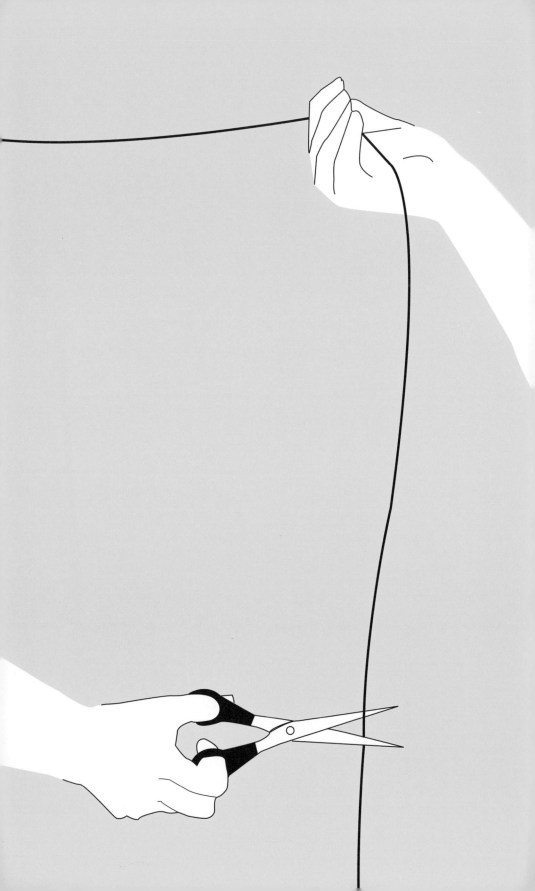

KARL
ON
LIFE

I am a witness. An egotistical member of the audience who's never tired of watching the world from the dress circle. So much the better if the dress circle has a good view. I'm more comfortable there than on the stage. Because today the show is in the auditorium. Sometimes it's dreadful, but never boring. I'd like to live for another 120 years to see the world evolve.

I don't like being watched at all. If I am being watched, I leave – because I'm playing a part 24 hours a day. Even to myself.

I build my own reality. I've created my own system that lets me sort out my life. I enjoy the luxury of being at the centre of this complete universe that's mine.

My autobiography?
I don't have to write it.

I'm living it.

For me, work is

CALM, COLD, ORGANIZED.

I hate hysteria.

*I hate holidays! That's for people who always
do the same thing in the same place. I spend my
time running from Milan to Paris to New York.
I work 20 hours a day, on my own initiative. I'm
the definition of the independent professional.*

*I'm arguing in favour of the 48-hour day.
I can't manage with just 24 hours.*

*When I was very young, at the beginning my
business was to work more than the others to
show them their pointlessness.*

*I'm not a serious person. Things come to me that
way. I work instinctively without asking myself
a mountain of questions.*

I know revenge is mean
and horrible, but I see
no reason why I shouldn't
do something back if somebody
has done something bad to me.

**When people think it's all
forgotten I pull the chair away
– maybe 10 years later.**

I've never smoked, never drunk, never taken drugs, but I don't tolerate sour-faced puritans and Calvinists. The opposite – I only like people who get high, who drink and smoke and do all the things I don't do. Some people are made to destroy themselves, and I admire that, but I'm made to survive. The survival instinct is my most advanced instinct. I only do the trapeze with a safety net.

Where do I get my energy? EDF (Envy, Desire and Forcefulness).

Psychoanalysis! First of all, it kills creativity. Secondly, if you are honest with yourself then you know all the questions and the answers. I don't need a psychoanalyst because I know the answers.

*I never drink anything hot; I don't like hot
drinks – very strange. I drink Diet Coke from
the minute I get up to the minute I go to bed,
and even in the middle of the night.*

*I never wanted to have children. Because if
a child didn't do as well as me, I wouldn't have
loved it, and if it did better than me I wouldn't
have loved it either.*

*If I were a woman I'd have children: but
I'm not a woman so that's the end of that.*

*My childhood dream was not to be a child.
I'd find it humiliating to be a child.
Second-class human being.*

I still have the furniture from my bedroom when I was a child. They are the only things I kept after my parents died. One day, when I'm a little old man, and I've shrunk, I will live with the sofa, the chest of drawers, the chairs, the table I used for writing and drawing ... and I'll sleep in my childhood bed.

I'm surrounded by young and beautiful people. I hate looking at ugliness.

I like to surround myself with music, books and paper, to make sketches and to think about everything deeply. To brainwash myself and write letters. I never feel alone. For me, solitude is when you are old, sick, poor, with no one around. But if you're quite well known and you have some money, that's the height of luxury. You have to fight for it ...

I don't like being an actor because my whole life is already a pantomime.

When I was younger I wanted to be a caricaturist. In the end I've become a caricature.

Every morning I have my little fifteen minutes of styling: I set up the puppet. It's a deep form of professional conditioning.

I'm fine living by myself – it's the ultimate luxury.

I like that the people who follow me in the street, who want photos with me, are very, very young. It's been my biggest success in life.

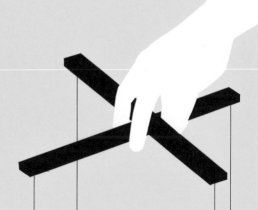

The personality
I project
to the media
is a puppet.
IT'S ME
PULLING
THE STRINGS.
The most important
thing is for the
strings to be
well tied.

People can say
and write what they
like about me, almost,
because I work
on the principle

**'SAY
WHAT
YOU
LIKE,
AS
LONG
AS
IT'S
NOT
TRUE.'**

I prefer to see and interpret the world from my window. Then I travel to see if what is really there is as interesting as what is in my mind.

I don't have any problems. It's my life's miracle. There are no problems, just solutions – good or bad.

Today I live by myself. I always see myself next to me. So there are always two of us, with one making fun of the other, who sees things clearly.

My life is science fiction. In any case, the gap between what people think they know about my life and reality is a matter of science fiction. Reality is something else … and it's much less fun.

Going for dinner in town is not my thing. Anyway, people don't ask me over, for fear I'll judge them, perhaps.

I don't want friends for the bad days. I find it distasteful. I want friends for the good days. The rest I'll manage on my own.

I have one instinct that is stronger than all the others: the survival instinct.

I don't need to shop for food because I never eat.

Apart from sketching, talking and reading, there's not much I can do. I mean, I know how to open a fridge, but I don't know how to cook.

PEOPLE WHO TELL ALL APPAL ME

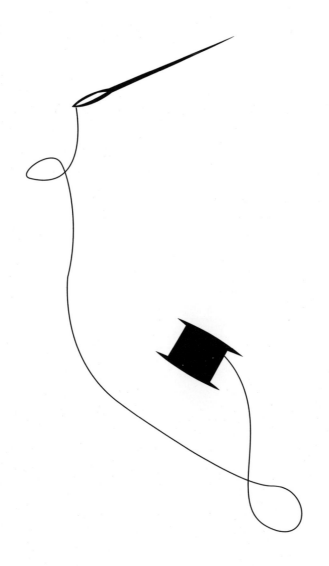

KARL
ON
FASHION

I love the
EPHEMERAL:
fashion
IS
MY PROFESSION.

I hate people in this profession who get stuck in a particular era and who think the world is going mad. The world isn't wrong, it's changing.

Fashion is of the moment. The best thing that can happen to a dress is that it gets worn. Fashion isn't about museum exhibits.

I like spending lots of money on clothes, because I make clothes and I earn lots of money from clothes. The others have to make money, too.

When you hear designers complaining about the challenge of their profession, you have to say: don't get carried away – **IT'S ONLY DRESSES.**

Trendy is the last stage before tacky.

In fashion you always have to break something to make it again, to love what you've hated and hate what you've loved.

Fashion is superficial. You have to accept that's how it is if you decide to choose it as a profession.

I remember a designer who said her dresses were worn only by intelligent women. Naturally she went bankrupt.

What fashion expresses doesn't last. Style lasts. But it has to follow fashion to outlive it.

You could say fashion creates trends, elegance follows fashions.

Times have changed, criteria change: there's no fashion aristocracy any more.

Fashion is the spirit you give things to make them evolve.

Every era gets the fashion it deserves.

*If you ask me what I'd most like to have invented in fashion, I'd say **the white shirt.** For me, the shirt is the basis of everything. Everything else comes after.*

Loving fashion means wearing it too.

*Fashion is an attitude more than a
clothing detail.*

*Fashion is like the ocean, or love: it comes
and goes like a wave.*

*Young designers are nice, but often they have no
technical knowledge. Valentino and I sweated
for years, he at Dessès, me at Balmain. We knew
we weren't there to play art critics, we were there
to learn.*

Fashion is like music: there are so many notes.... You need to play around with them. We all have to make our own tune.

Fashion is a game

*that has to be
played seriously.*

Fashion is neither moral nor amoral – but it can boost your morale.

Fashion? Well, everything is fashion!

Fashion is made up of two things: continuity and the opposite. That's why you have to keep moving.

The world of fashion is ephemeral, dangerous and unfair.

KARLISMS
1

Happiness is not a given. It takes work and it requires some effort.

There was a time when people knew how to be serious and lighthearted, earnest and witty all at once. Times have changed.

Every era gets the bad taste it deserves.

There was a time when so-called 'high society' people would phone each other's servants. Now they're the ones being phoned non-stop and they think they have to pick up that second if possible, as if they were working on the switchboard of a big hotel during high season at rush hour.

The only thing that
lasts is the ephemeral.
THE FRAGILITY
OF LIFE
AND FASHION
suits me
very well.

*You have to have the courage of what you've
been convicted of.*

⌇

*Art is something you feel. You don't need
to own it.*

⌇

*Working is when you do a job you don't like.
The minute you like your job, it's not working
any more.*

⌇

*People in politics have a problem. If they are too
well dressed, it's a problem. If they are not well
dressed, it's a problem too. So they have to find
the borderline; it's not easy.*

⌇

*To be able to adapt to all the highs, you have to
know all the lows as well.*

Ugliness has evolved; internal ugliness matters more than external ugliness.

The important thing is not to be connected on every level – it's to be well connected.

You must never be afraid of progress. Otherwise you are damned.

To think appearances don't count these days is a lie: it lets you live in harmony with yourself.

Personality begins where comparison ends.

THE MINK IS A VERY DANGEROUS ANIMAL THAT HATES MAN.

*Frustration is the mother of crime. I'm afraid
there would be much more crime if it weren't for
prostitutes and porno films.*

*If you're too tidy you'll never find anything.
You'll never be surprised, or know the delights
of finding things by chance.*

*Homosexuality is like hair colour, nothing more.
And then it avoids the problem of having an
unbearable daughter-in-law, my mother
used to say.*

*Spitefulness is excusable if it's spiritual.
If it's gratuitous, it's unforgivable.*

No deadline for a new life.

Change is the healthiest way to survive.

*There is nothing worse than bringing up the
'good old days'. To me, that's the ultimate
acknowledgement of failure.*

*Whining about one's past is the beginning
of a lack of future.*

*The minute you think that the past was better,
your present is second hand, and you become
vintage – it's OK for clothes, not that great
for people.*

*Life isn't a beauty contest. Intelligence lasts,
youth and beauty are seasonal.*

*When you're young you are always a bit of
an idiot. What saves us is that we realize it later.*

*Youth is just for hire: those who have it
are going to lose it tomorrow.*

*Youth is an invention of middle-aged people
to make others feel older.*

*Youth is a club from which every member
will be excluded one day.*

Whenever you have a success, you have to pay for it next time. Whatever you do, people will say: 'Oh! It wasn't as good as the last time.' Then you do a few more and it's all good again. Memories make things seem even greater than they were. You have to know that.

The obsession with rock stars is great, because even people who didn't like jeans and rock music think they look like rock stars in jeans now.

When people want to be loved for what they have done, they should stop.

You have to do things that one is not supposed to do.

Think pink

AS DIANA VREELAND SAID – BUT DON'T WEAR IT.

KARL
ON
STYLE

When I hear old fools say 'elegance is dead',
I tell them: 'no it's not, its face has changed'.

If you don't have an elegant physique,
the most elegant dress won't change that.
An Ethiopian peasant can be madly elegant,
and a very rich person may look like a pint pot.

Elegance isn't about having a well-stocked
closet, or a well-stocked wallet.

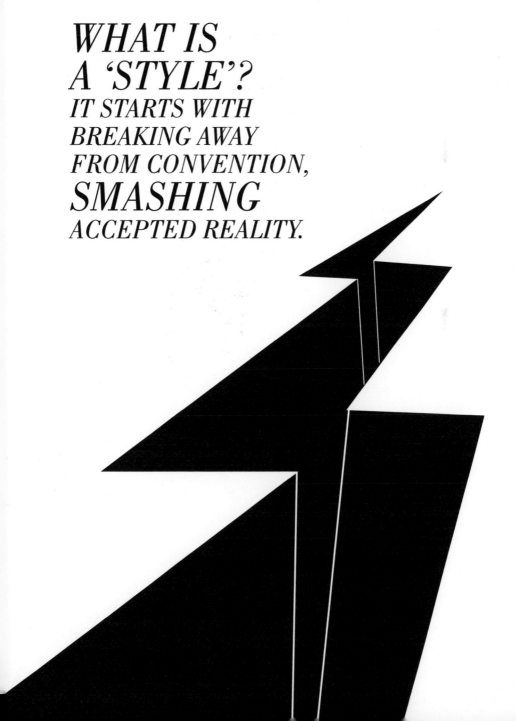

WHAT IS A 'STYLE'?
IT STARTS WITH BREAKING AWAY FROM CONVENTION,
SMASHING
ACCEPTED REALITY.

The clothes don't have to suit you; you have to suit the clothes.

Elegance is an attitude, a way of moving.
It's not a patented idea: over the years, ambitions
and ideas change.

Today, I think of elegance as a moral or
physical phenomenon, not something to do
with fabrics, cosmetics or perfume.

There comes a time in life when the idea of
beauty and youth has to give way to style
and elegance.

'To be distinguished': it's dull, that expression,
not modern at all, something a clerk would say:
'The lady is very distinguished.' I don't want
to be distinguished at all. But I don't mind if
people distinguish me.

Having style is about being at ease with the life around us. Because what's fun, in the end, is to be of one's time.

⌀

Summer clothes that are rumpled or relaxed drive me mad. I loathe 'rumpledness', if I can put it that way. It's OK between the ages of 25 and 30, but unfortunately after that it's dreadful. I hate people in the street who look like they've raided their grandchildren's wardrobe.

⌀

Jogging pants are a sign of defeat. You've lost control of your life, so you go out in jogging pants.

⌀

I'd like to have a nose with a bump. It's very chic.

One is
never
underdressed
or overdressed
with a
**Little
Black
Dress**
or a
**Little
Black
Jacket**.

KARL
ON
KARL

1

I am a black and white person.

⌒

I am a trapeze artist with a very strong safety net. I have a hint of vulnerability, but it's foreign to me.

⌒

To be happy? No, I'm not so ambitious.

⌒

I'm not like Chamfort, who worked on his witticisms in the morning before he went out.

⌒

I'm a kind of hired gun, so if the army is good it's OK, but if the army is not good there is little I can do.

I
AM

a walking meringue

my own iPad

a one-off

a very good scanner

here to do, not to have done

less horrible than I seem

entirely at my disposal

born to be alone

I AM A
BLACK DIAMOND,
UNFACETED.
BLACK DIAMONDS
ARE RARE,
HARD TO CUT,
AND THEREFORE
UNCOMMERCIAL.

*It's not that I think I'm good, but it could
be worse.*

*I didn't come up with my character. It's a series
of evolutions and chance events that produce it.
It's not something I thought about.*

*I like the idea that people think I'm wicked.
I think I'm a bit of a chump.*

*I'm never happy. I'm in a permanent state
of dissatisfaction.*

With wordplay you've got me. I just love it.

I feel no remorse and no regrets. I have amnesia when it comes to the past.

In fact, I'm an old literature teacher – except I don't give lessons. That's it: I'm my own teacher and my curiosity grows with age.

My contracts are for life. I'm condemned to death, condemned to life.

I've nothing to pass on, I'm a complete sham.

Normal people think I'm insane.

I am a living label.
My name is

LABELFELD

not Lagerfeld.

I am like
a caricature
of myself.
*LIKE A
MASK.*
For me, the
Carnival of
Venice lasts
all year.

I am in an endlessly bad mood with myself.

I am the king of the iPod!

I've been around for so long, prehistoric man can't compete.

I am present and absent at the same time.

I'm puritanical ... but it doesn't show too much.

I'll be puritanical to the day I die: I don't like alcohol, I don't like drugs, and I've never been obsessed with sex. I'm a paragon of virtue, an undeserving paragon of virtue.

I am in favour of the general opinion of one person only.

With me there's nothing below the surface. It's quite a surface.

I am an inhabitant of nowhere. I am a free European.

I am three people. When I speak English I'm one person; when I speak German I'm another; and when I speak French I'm somebody else again.

I am a total improvisation.

I have no wish to be normal.

I
am

modesty itself.

KARL
ON
CHANEL

Chanel's success was knowing how to get across the elements of her identity. Timeless music built around five notes by which women instantly recognize the essence of Chanel: luxury and refinement.

I try to evolve the Chanel style by thinking of Goethe's phrase: make a better future by building on the past.

In the end, I am just a mercenary paid to perpetuate the label. You can't go wrong with that.

Chanel left us with something better than fashion: style. And style, as she preached it, doesn't grow old.

I juggle with what I know and what I don't know about her.

She invented something:
she invented the 'total look'.
She was the first to want
a 'woman's perfume with a
woman's scent', for herself alone.
Jewels for her collection.
From hats to shoes, from
chain-belts to camellias, from
bows to bags, she transformed
the accessory, she turned
**the trivial into
the essential.**

In the 1930s she was much better known for her lace dresses than for her suits. If you say lace, I think of Chanel. Lace: 'dentelle', Chanel … it rhymes.

My favourite Coco Chanel is the one at the beginning. The rebellious one, the whimsical one, who cut her hair one evening before a first night at the opera, because a water heater blew up and singed her superb hair. I love her wickedness when she was funny, her intelligence. It's her I think about when I'm designing my collections.

What I've done, Coco Chanel would never have done. She would have hated it.

I adore Chanel

but it's not me.

Chanel was a woman of her times. She wasn't a backward-looking has-been. The opposite – she hated the past, including her own past, and her whole thing comes from that. That's why the Chanel brand has to be the image of the moment.

I know Chanel's DNA thoroughly, and it's strong enough not to have to talk about it.

The idea of Chanel was to become a decent lady. But there is a moment when decency becomes boredom – and I have to fight against boredom. I have to work it out so that I give an image of Chanel that is fun, that is for today, that is unrelated to the past, because the past is an idea. To respect the past as a reality is something that will kill you.

People tend to forget that there was a time when Chanel was through. The only people who wore Chanel were doctors' wives living in the 16th [arrondissement]. No one would go near it: it was hopeless.

Chanel herself had style, but she wasn't truly elegant – that was her tragedy.

Was Coco Chanel wicked? Not with men, anyway. She was a trickster, a charmer second to none. On the other hand, Chanel hated women, she said they were dirty and untidy…

I'm a funny sort of Coco.

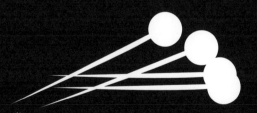

A touch of humour and a bit of disrespect: that's what a legend needs to survive.

Chanel is a look that can be adapted to every era, to every age range. It's the elements of a wardrobe, like jeans, the T-shirt, the white shirt. The Chanel jacket is like the two-button suit for a man.

Mademoiselle's genius is to have introduced the suit, the camellia or the gold chain as though she'd invented them. A bit like Charlie Chaplin with his walking stick, his moustache and his hat.

Chanel's style is an ego trip. She did everything for herself. To assert herself. I understand that very well.

[My cat] Choupette isn't a typical Chanel woman. She's more Jean Harlow.

My work is not to make the Chanel suit survive, but to make sure **it lives.**

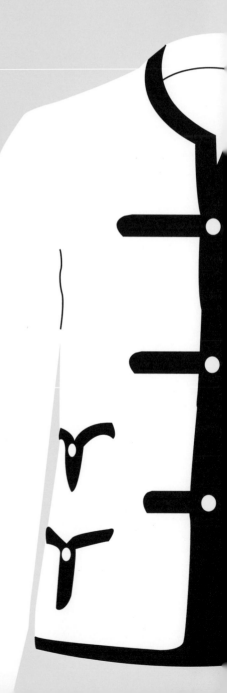

KARL
ON
LUXURY

You have to lead your life according to your ideas. Spend all your money and live life in line with what you are fighting for. I hate it when rich people try to be Communists. I think that's obscene.

If you throw your money out of the window, do it with passion. Don't say 'you shouldn't do that', that's bourgeois.

LUXURY
IS A
DISCIPLINE

Often these days
**LUXURY IS
EXPENSIVE
GOODIES BOUGHT
BY NOBODIES**
*who don't have
a luxury life.*

*Luxury is freedom of spirit, independence,
basically political incorrectness.*

*The essential thing is not that people should
sit on their money. It has to come out of
their pockets.*

*What is this obsession always to be with people?
Solitude is the biggest luxury.*

What's fun is collecting, not owning. But to get rid of things you have to have owned things. People who have never had money and say they don't like it don't know what it is. As for those who have it and don't like it they should give it back! Money is made to go round, not to bring in more money. I like people who live beyond their means, who throw money out of the window, adventurers. The danger is rich people being afraid and not spending it.

I hate rich people who live within their means.

MY GREATEST LUXURY IS NOT TO HAVE TO JUSTIFY MYSELF TO ANYONE.

KARL
ON
BEING *IN*
SHAPE

*I worked out a lot
before I was 20. I was hard
underneath. I had just a little
padding. I was quilted.
Always Chanel…*

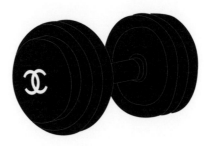

For me the height of luxury is to have an extra slice of toast. It's the most delicious thing in the world.

At my age, I don't need to be a pack of sexy muscle, thank you very much. Now it's better to ask yourself what you look like dressed rather than undressed.

I've rediscovered all my muscles and I could have a beach body, but it's not my role any more.

*I didn't go on this diet for people to paw me
or to be sexy. I wanted to be a good coat hanger.*

*I wanted to be a perfect coat hanger for
slim-fitting clothes.*

*I think that for both women and men fashion
is the healthiest motivation for losing weight.*

I
WANT
TO
BE
A
CHIC
COAT HANGER

MY ONLY AMBITION IN LIFE IS TO WEAR SIZE 30 JEANS.

At Dior, or even at other houses, they've never altered so much as a button for me.

Buy clothes in the size you want to wear. Get rid of the rest, give it away, and when you have no more clothes I can guarantee that if you are a kilo overweight, you'll make an effort. Because there's nothing more unpleasant than a pair of trousers that fit a bit too tightly.

I am like those bidets and sinks: Ideal Standard.

In France, they talk about the Ancien Régime. My regime isn't ancien, it's always up to date.

No one wants to see curvy women up there. You've got fat mothers sitting in front of the television with their bags of chips and saying thin models are ugly. Fashion is about dreams and illusions.

Models are thin, yes, but they're not 'so' thin.

Yes, some people say to me 'you're too skinny'. But a skinny person never says that to me, only people who could lose a few pounds say that.

A diet is the only game where you win while you're losing.

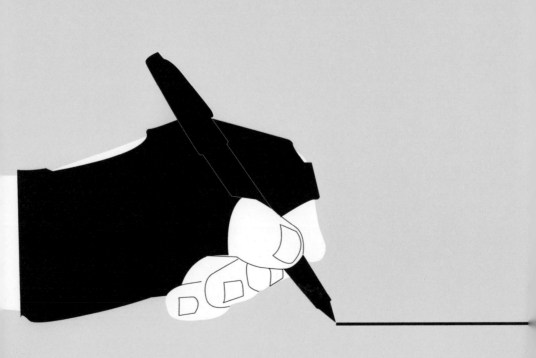

KARL
ON
DESIGN

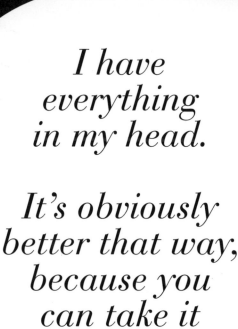

I have everything in my head.

It's obviously better that way, because you can take it everywhere.

*Influence is something in the air. I'm like
a TV aerial.*

*I feed off everything. I'm a satellite dish that
picks up everything, processes everything, and
reconstitutes it.*

*I am my own computer, and I memorize
everything I see. I have thousands of references.*

*Whatever's in the air at the time, my role is
to propose, not impose; what women do after
is up to them.*

I like to undo in order to redo. That's my motor.

I never learned
to draw. That came
by itself. I don't
understand not
knowing how
to draw.

*Everything in life that I've done well I've seen
while I was asleep. That's why I always keep
a sketchpad close to my bed.*

*My best ideas come to me when I'm asleep.
That's the drama and the happiness of my life.
I don't know where they come from. That's what
I live off: the unconscious made real.*

*I don't do anything in relation to other people.
I only do things in relation to myself.*

You only design by going against received ideas.

I never fall in love. I'm in love with my jobs.

You have to feel what women want. It's like a game, a challenge.

I don't remember anything. My trick is to burn everything and start again from zero.

I throw everything away. The most important piece of furniture is the garbage can. I keep no archives.

Because I'm never satisfied, which is my real drama and good fortune, as soon as one collection is over I only think about designing the next.

I do my job like I breathe. So if I don't breathe I'm in trouble.

I am supposed **to do.**

I'm not supposed to remember.

I like **doing**

— not flaunting what I have done.

My life consists of forgetting what I have **done.**

I'm open to anything. For me, everything that is in accordance with the

zeitgeist

is OK.

Design as art is contrived. Designing clothes is working-class: I'm working-class.

I don't believe too much in advice. I never got any, so I don't give any.

I don't analyse what I do. I do it without comment. I propose things. My life is a life of proposals.

The purpose of dress design is to make people feel good, not to express the pain and the suffering of the world in taffeta.

*The keyword of our profession is 'desire'.
You have to create a desire.*

*I draw just as I breathe. You don't breathe
to order. It just happens by itself.*

*Designers who get all serious, I find that mind-
numbing and ridiculous. Making dresses is
important, but they're only dresses. You're not
Kierkegaard after all.*

*In this profession you have to shut up and work.
Do things intuitively. I'm not a marketing person,
I'm someone who draws what I see and hopes that
it will come out right. I hate pseudo-intellectual
conversations about fashion. Fashion is what's
worn in the street.*

When I do something,
I do it 100 per cent.
I'm a professional
killer.

KARL
ON
BEING
CONTROVERSIAL

*I am a kind of fashion nymphomaniac
who never gets an orgasm. I am never satisfied.*

*I don't like having people over. They can come,
but when evening comes they have to leave.
I hate promiscuity.*

*When people irritate me, I say anything.
I like being politically incorrect as well,
because I can't put up with political
correctness.*

*I hate double-talk. If I say something unkind
about people, it's when they've done something
to me, however long ago, which in my opinion
gives me the right to have a go at them for fun
whenever I like.*

I ALWAYS SAY WHAT I THINK,

AND SOMETIMES EVEN WHAT I DON'T THINK

I hate intellectuals, especially if they are not very well dressed. Look at photos of people like **BERGSON:** *impeccable!*

Today they are all *A LITTLE SLOPPY*.

I didn't become a designer to talk a lot of hot air, and massage my own ego churning out unwearable and cranky collections. It's fundamental for me that women wear what I design and that they want to own it.

If I was a Russian woman I'd be a lesbian. Russian men are really not very good-looking.

It's always been my dream to have white hair. Dry shampoo is my cocaine.

With everything there is to see, do, know, read, how can one ever be fed up? That means you must be a fool.

❧

[French employment minister] Martine Aubry is right: you can't do a job that bores you rigid for more than 35 hours.

❧

Do I know how much I have in my bank account? That's a question for people with little money.

❧

Eras get what they deserve. We've got the telephone, which is the most ill-mannered thing in the world. Today people have three phones in front of them, and they ring, people ring them, like maids! Myself included.

I've never voted in my life. I never will. I know only too well the way politics work. Reading newspapers puts you off too.... To vote you have to believe all the promises they make, which they won't keep. But if you give me an Obama button, I don't mind wearing it.

When people show their ass that doesn't bother me. When they expose their feelings, that shocks me.

I say what I think, because I'm a free European.

I hate intellectual conversations.

I'm only interested in my own opinion.

Apart from one assistant I only work with women. I have only ever had trouble working with men, because at any given moment they think they're better than me. They get egocentric and think to themselves that if I can do it, they can too.

Men who have worked with me must have been terribly frustrated … not to be me. It's horrible what I'm saying, but lots of men or boys have thought they were more gifted than me, and they all failed. I don't have that problem with women.

My mother said she had never been a feminist, because she wasn't ugly enough for that.

My sunglasses are my burka for men.

When I was a child I was sent to Kitzbühel with my older sister, who went off screwing with the instructor while I got bored to death. Since that day I swore I'd never take part in winter sports again.

Haute couture for women is often cosmetic surgery – high fashion, since everything has to be lifted.

There's no justice. Social injustice is almost the only kind you can cure. When a girl is ugly and has a fat ass down to the ground, what can you do? She'll never be Claudia Schiffer – that's real injustice.

I HAVE
NO HUMAN
FEELINGS.

KARL
LAGERFELD

KARL
ON
CELEBRITY

I will never write my memoirs. Because I have nothing to say, and I would have to mention people I don't want to talk about.

If I've become more visible than some of my colleagues maybe it's because I have a big mouth. My celebrity has almost nothing to do with my profession.

If I had to write them, I'd publish my memoirs after my death; before that I can't, I've got too many scores to settle.

I don't want to be a reality in other people's lives. I want to be like an apparition, appearing and disappearing.

*I'VE
BECOME
LIKE A
LACOSTE
ALLIGATOR.*

*Soon I'll have
to be sewn
onto clothes.*

KARLISMS
2

I hate time passing.

I hate small men. They're the most wicked, bitter and vindictive kind there is.

I like the idea of craziness with discipline.

*I hate ostrich skin.
It makes me think
of a mummy that
had regular acne.*

There's nothing more mind-numbing than people who talk too much

– that's why I prefer silent movies.

I don't like animals being massacred, but I don't like human beings being massacred either, and apparently it's rather popular in the world.

I have a preference for silent movies. I don't like loud talking.

Energy should always be new. There is no old energy. You cannot stock energy. You can for electricity but not for creativity.

I hate TV at home. Seeing human beings who don't exist in the house makes me afraid. I don't want melodrama and tragedy invading my universe, which is completely antiseptic and serene.

I don't like the word 'antiques' – especially when it's applied to people.

In the truly vulgar there is always something truthful that I find touching.

The essential thing in life is to reinvent oneself.

Eras are what they are. It's for us to adapt, not for the era to adapt to us. It's not made to measure.

My motto is that there's no credit in the past. To have done something is of no interest.

When you are shortsighted, the first ten minutes after you take your glasses off you look like a rescue dog that wants to be taken to the pound. That's not my look. That's why I wear dark glasses.

Real social injustice is youth. It's a little club that no one belongs to for life.

I skate on very thin ice, and I have to keep going before it cracks.

I am not a fortune-teller. I am a fashion tailor.

For me, interesting people are the ones who do something that I can't.

What interests me is not reality, but my idea of it.

Homage and respect can paralyse you. I'm here to reset the clock.

I love goddesses because they were the first liberated women, who were free to do anything. Divinities and muses are feminists!

What I love about my work is the work.

WHAT DO I LIKE
ABOUT PHOTOS?

THEY EVOKE A STATE
THAT'S IMPOSSIBLE
TO REPRODUCE,
GONE FOREVER.

KARL
ON
BOOKS

I have always read a lot and I still read a lot. But I don't like to flaunt it or talk about it. If people think I'm stupid, superficial, I don't care. They think what they like.

◦ℐ◦

I read up to twenty books at once.

◦ℐ◦

Reading is the biggest luxury in my life, the thing that makes me happiest.

◦ℐ◦

Books are my blood and my world. I've always understood passion for books and being obsessed by them. I know what they can do to you. Storing them forever and enjoying their company is always reassuring.

I DON'T READ TO TALK ABOUT IT

– I hate intellectual conversations.

JUST TO KNOW.

BOOKS ARE A HARD-BOUND DRUG ON WHICH YOU CAN'T OVERDOSE.

I am the happy
victim of books.

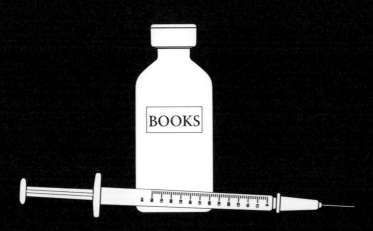

Buying books is a real disease for me, but
I don't want to be cured.

With every book you buy you should be able
to buy the time to read it, Schopenhauer said.

I cannot live without books. The room is dead
if there are no books.

The smell of a book is the best smell in the world.

I am crazy about books. Books are the tragedy
and the happiness of my life.

I'm a willing victim of books.

*I love contemporary art, but I don't want
any at home. At home I want only books.*

*I have three jobs. Fashion, photography
and books. They all inspire me.*

*In spite of my schedule, I'm always reading,
driven by a permanent guilty conscience that
makes it even better. I live surrounded by books.
You'll see at my home, you'll understand how
serious it is.*

*For me, reading is a serious illness,
a pathological obsession!*

I'm a slave to my books.

I WANT
to read
everything,
to see everything,
to be informed.

I am a
PAPER ADDICT,
a PAPER FREAK,
a PAPER-WORM.

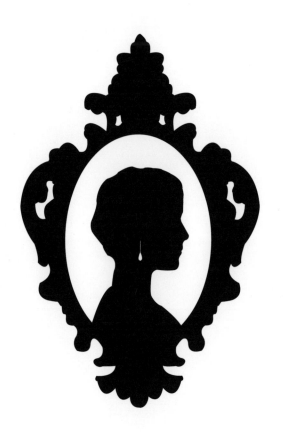

ELISABETH
ON
KARL

*I had the parents
I needed:*

A FATHER
who let me do everything

AND

A MOTHER
*who put me in my place
and gave me a clip
round the ear.*

My mother would say to me: 'You have to leave Hamburg. Here you could get to be a drawing teacher – but I didn't go through nine months of pregnancy for that.'

When it comes to elegance for men, my mother would always give two Germans as examples, Count Kessler and Walther Rathenau: 'Those are great people. The rest, forget it. They're nothing.'

My mother said: 'I admire what you're doing because it proves you're not a snob. Nobody who is snob would do a job like this – you have underused all your possibilities.'

When I was 11 years old, I asked my mother what homosexuality was. She said: 'It's not important. It's like hair colour: some are blonde, some are brunette.'

I'm always late, it's the tragedy of my life. I was born three weeks after I was due. My mother said that she went to the clinic every day because she didn't want the 'mess' at home. I never got those three weeks back.

I loved hats when I was a child. I'd wear Tyrolean hats, and my mother – I was something like eight – said to me: 'You shouldn't wear hats. You look like an old dyke.' She was quite funny, no?

*I was born in
a port city,
Hamburg.
My mother
would say:*

*'It's the gateway
to the world,
but it's only
the gateway.
So get out
of here!'*

*MY MOTHER
TRIED TO GET
ME TO PLAY
THE PIANO.
ONE DAY SHE
SHUT THE
PIANO LID
ON MY FINGERS
AND SAID:*

**'DRAW!
IT MAKES
LESS NOISE.'**

*Another time, my mother said on the subject
of men: 'You can make a child with any man.
One shouldn't overstate their importance.'*

*When she broke up with a lover, I was told my
mother said: 'He wasn't needed any more for
my spiritual evolution.'*

*Only being interested in yourself lets you be
more available for others. My mother said:
'You should never sacrifice yourself too much
because afterwards you'll have nothing more to
give. So think about yourself, then you can be
interested in others and be useful.'*

*My mother also said: 'I'm going to have to take
you to the upholsterer. Your nostrils are too big –
they need curtains.'*

All my life, she would say to me:

'You look like me, but much less nice.'

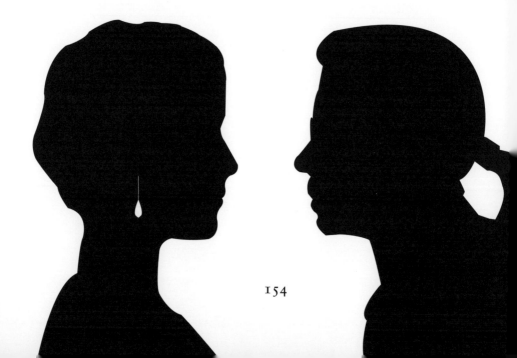

*My mother thought the most important thing
in life was to be skinny. When she visited me in
Paris, she would tell me: 'It's a pity you can't see
yourself from behind. You have a big backside.'*

*When I was 14 I wanted to be like my mother,
who smoked like a chimney. I wanted to smoke
to play at being grown up. My mother said to
me: 'You shouldn't smoke. Your hands aren't so
pretty, and when you smoke it attracts attention
to them.'*

*I remember my mother telephoned me on my
24th birthday. She said: 'Oh, by the way:
after 24 it's downhill. So you'd better pay
attention from now on. You can say goodbye
to your youth.'*

When I was a child my hair would sometimes stick up at the sides. One day my mother said to me: 'You know what you look like? A Strasbourg pot.' You know, with those ridiculous handles...

My mother would always say: 'When you're talking rubbish, speak more quickly, we don't have time to waste.' And she would get up and head for the door.

When my father died, my mother sold the house and sent me the furniture from my room, which I still have. I said to her: 'But my journal was in the desk!' And she replied: 'I threw it out. Is it really so essential for the world to know you were an idiot?'

My mother had great nerve.

In comparison I'm a shrinking violet.

KARL
ON
KARL
2

The last thing I'd do is define myself. Tomorrow I could be the opposite of what I am today.

What do I know how to do? Nothing. Talk a little, draw a little. I have some vague ideas, and thank God people help me realize them. I've never studied and I don't have a qualification.

I'm as old as my face.

In one sense, I'm ageless, I don't belong to any generation.

If there's one thing that I'm miles away from, it's political correctness.

How old am I?

Everyone knows that I'm

100 years old

– so it doesn't matter.

I don't recommend myself as a guest.

I wouldn't incite someone to crime, but I'm not making any effort to help others survive.

I may be scary to some people but not to me. I know what is behind the black glasses.

I'm not in the least complacent towards myself. But I'm always very forgiving of other people. Because I'm only interested in myself, or rather in the things I do. And absolutely not in other people.

A fortune-teller told my mother that I would become a priest, but my mother didn't want that to happen. So I wasn't allowed to go to churches. I never went to a marriage or a burial throughout my childhood. Not even a Christmas service.

*I stopped thinking anything about myself
a long time ago.*

*From the moment I agree with myself I can
make of myself whatever I want.*

*I don't mind being a monster, but there
are limits.*

*The most important thing you should know
about me is that not everything you're told
by others is necessarily the truth.*

*I like it that people don't seem nice and that
you can discover them. I never smile either,
I find that inane.*

I've gone beyond

ego.

The mother of all crimes is frustration, and I'm not at all frustrated.

For people like me, solitude is a victory, it's a struggle.

I've always had excess baggage.

I'm always busy. You know, the more I do, the more ideas I have – that's the funny thing. The brain is a muscle, and I'm a kind of body-builder.

The emotions expressed by the eyes, they're not something I really want to put on the market. That's why I wear dark glasses.

It's my puritan nature that sustains me. It doesn't have much to do with my education, but a lot with MY PRUSSIAN BACKBONE: you can't jump over your own shadow...

Maybe I'm better
on answers
than on questions.

There is one thing I love on earth: to learn.

There are perhaps five people in the world whose criticism I care about. The others, it's their opinion and I couldn't care less.

I'm never pleased with myself, I always think I could do better, that I'm lazy, that I don't make enough effort.

I like to know things, to know everything. To be informed. I'm a kind of universal 'concierge', not an intellectual.

I never wear glasses at home. I don't need to.

*I have a
client mentality.
I like to shop.*

I still like to give the image of superficiality.
I do not want to be serious. I like to say stupid
things and I like to behave as if I was a silly,
superficial person because nothing is more
boring than an intellectual, a heavy message.
I am not a message-giver.

I never go out without my notorious dark glasses.
I like to see, not to be observed.

I like everything to be washable, myself included.

I've always known I was made to live this way, that I would be this sort of legend.

I don't mind being kind, but it mustn't show.

I only know how to play one role: me.

I'm not going to calm down, because that's not my nature.

I hate the idea of lumbering people with whatever's left. When it's over, it's over. I'm against memory. There comes a time when you have to pack it in. I admire the animals in the wild. When they die you don't see them again.

I'm like
perishable goods:

what I say
doesn't keep.

SOURCES

MEDIA, PRESS AND BOOKS

Air France magazine • Another Mag • Art Auction • Bazaar • Connaissance des Arts • Daily Telegraph • Depeche Mode • Die Zeit • Elle • Elle UK • Elle Decoration India • France 2 • France 3 • Glass • GQ • ID magazine • Independent Style Magazine • Infolunettes • InStyle • L'Express • L'Officiel de la Mode • Le Figaro • Le Figaro Madame • Le Figaro Magazine • Le Parisien • Le Point • Le Temps de la Mode • Les Échos • Les Inrockuptibles • Libération • Libération Next • M le Magazine • Magazine • Marie-Claire • Metro • Mirabella • Mixte • New York Times Style Magazine • Newsweek • New York Magazine • Numéro • Observer Magazine • Obsession • Paris Capitale • Série Limitée • Stiletto spécial Chanel • Tatler • Télérama • The Times Luxx Magazine • Town and Country • Vice • Vogue Australia • Vogue France • VSD • W Magazine – Ykone • Zeitung Magazin • The Karl Lagerfeld Diet

DOCUMENTARIES AND INTERVIEWS

Canal + • CNN • Interview with Frédéric Beigbeder • Europe 1 • France 2 • France Inter • Gulfnews.com • Interviews by Alexandra Golovanoff • Karl.com • Karl Lagerfeld se dessine (Loïc Prigent, 2013) • Lagerfeld Confidential (Rodolphe Marconi, 2007) • Paris Première • Programme Nijinsky 2004 • RTL • TF1 • ZDF

ABOUT THE AUTHORS

Patrick Mauriès, author and publisher, has written more than thirty works. He has known Karl Lagerfeld since the beginning of his literary career.
Jean-Christophe Napias is an author, translator and editor.